*Then and Now*
*Love Lost and Sometimes Found*

**ORI Z. SOLTES** teaches at Georgetown University across a range of disciplines, from theology and art history to philosophy and political history. He has also taught at Johns Hopkins University, Cleveland State University, Siegel College, and Case Western Reserve University. Soltes has lectured at dozens of museums, including the Metropolitan Museum of Art, the National Gallery of Art, the Smithsonian Institution, the Art Institute of Chicago, and the Los Angeles County Museum of Art. He is the former director and curator of the B'nai B'rith Klutznick National Jewish Museum, Washington, DC, where he curated over eighty exhibitions. Soltes has authored scores of books, articles, exhibition catalogs, and essays on diverse topics, including *Our Sacred Signs: How Jewish, Christian and Muslim Art Draw from the Same Source*; *Mysticism in Judaism, Christianity, and Islam: Searching for Oneness*; and *Tradition and Transformation: Three Millennia of Jewish Art and Architecture.*

§

The fascinating dynamic of Ori Soltes'
poems is that he's let the American
language bring to the classical Greek
and biblical Hebraic situations and
personae that obsess him, as well as his
own personal drama, not simply a
contemporary poetic presence but also
the contradictions between living and
dead worlds that makes one want
to speak of his poems as Presente! in
the highest sense of that word.

Jack Hirschman, San Francisco's Poet-
Laureate, author of *The Arcanes*,
*Liripol*, and *All That's Left*

§

Some poets write with their blood;
others grace us with inspirations
written out with their piss or spit or
other excreta. Soltes writes with his
eyes, with his mind whispering
Catullus-like chiseled observations
that comb the horizons of history, of
literature, of human dignity and love
within the drama, the tragicomedy,
the farce and the circus, but also the
rare exquisiteness and quixotic
intellection.

Alex S. Kohav, philosopher, artist,
poet, author of *The Sôd Hypothesis*
and editor of *Mysticism and Meaning:
Multidisciplinary Perspectives*

§

Such strikingly beautiful poetic
narratives. I re-read them trying to
penetrate their many layers of
meaning—the Hebrew, Greek,
Medieval: ancient voices in
communion and commonality,
sharing love, loss, friendship: the
captive mind of questionable and
unquestionable duty, regeneration—
continues to resonate. How beautiful
they are (to repeat)!

Gerald Wartofsky, painter

§

Taken together, the searching poetic
monologues of Ori Soltes' *Then and
Now: Love Lost and Sometimes
Found* deftly stitch together past and
present, myth and history, personal
stories and shared cultural narratives.
We hear myriad voices here—from
Antigone, Cain, and Gilgamesh,
among many others, to
representations of the author himself.
Wisdom both ancient and
contemporary rises from this chorus
of voices: we're all on a hero's
journey; we're all wrestling with the
stories that have defined us; we're all
painfully, deliciously real.

David Ebenbach, author of *We Were
the People Who Moved, Miss
Portland*, and other books

# Then and Now:
## Love Lost and Sometimes Found

### Ori Z. Soltes

○ CANAL STREET STUDIOS ○ NEW YORK ○

CANAL STREET STUDIOS new york
P.O. BOX 17722
BOULDER, CO 80308-0722

Soltes, Ori Z., 1951 –
*Then and Now: Love Lost and Sometimes Found*

ISBN-13: 978-0-9994594-0-9

1. Poetry  2. Ancient Israel
3. Ancient Greece  4. Title  5. Rome
6. Classics  7. Poetry—American

COVER IMAGES (*from top*):

*Achilles Slaying Penthesilea* (detail)
Penthesilea Painter
Attic Red-Figure kylix, ca 470-60 BCE, Munich Glyptotek

*Sarah's Lament*
Elaine Langerman
Mixed Media, 2013, Private Collection

For those who have taught me
different kinds of love:
my parents: Avraham and Sara;
my siblings: Eyton, Dafna, Michal, and Marnin;
my wife, Leslie;
and my sons, Brahm and Nadav:
...across the endless sky
of time.

# CONTENTS

## III. TIME BETWEEN TIME

## IV. SEASONS:
## THEN AND NOW

# FOREWORD

Some, like Santiago Ramon y Cajal, envision our interior landscape. He combined his exquisite artistic sense with an understanding a hundred years ahead of his time of the plasticity of the brain, that new synapses form throughout life as the basis for learning and memory.

Others, like Ori Soltes, journey across time and vast physical landscapes. His map has no boundaries. He is as much at home with Odysseus on his journey toward Troy as with Adam speaking in first person to his God about the burdens that attend mortality. What, asks the narrator in "Adam Mutters to His God," if I had chosen to avoid "that sweet fruit/ that suckled us"? Or was it that "His God" had "spread...the net/ whose filaments...//would set us free from You"—that the entry into finite life had nothing to do with choice or one's actions.

A nameless warrior cast in marble comes to life and love before our eyes in Soltes' poetry, as does the play between anonymous preservation and "our evanescence—//swiftly/ gone/ when measured/ by flesh,//not stone/and breath/that moves//in and out/in war/and love."

Our poet Soltes is fearless. He takes on the voice of Homer and argues across the centuries with well-meaning scholars—"They'll spew forth/tales fashioned/of catalogues of//notes—as many as/the warriors who sailed forth/ to rescue Helen//and were lost//They'll speculate:/if he wrote *one*//Did he also write/the *other*? As if/ a poem filled//with voices from the gods/could not speak twice:"

In the final section of the book, "Seasons: Then and Now," where the poems are largely contemporary, Ori Soltes continues to bring the power of myth and mortality to life. In "School Buses" which carry our precious cargo, the narrator asks: "do they have souls/

that know/ that they are/empty carapaces...when not/ the shepherds/ of their flocks?"

Whether it is Cajal's use of intricate drawings of neurons, or Ori Soltes's way of approaching this transformational journey through poetry, we are brought—in his words—to a new "sense of our own glorious possibilities, our flaws and limitations... [our] struggle against what we intrinsically are toward what we wish to be." And we are all the better for it.

— Myra Sklarew,
Professor of Literature at American University;
recipient of National Jewish Book Council Award,
the Di Castagnola Award,
and the PEN Syndicated Fiction Award

# 1. Ancient Hebrews and Israelites

# Adam Mutters to His God

— and if
we didn't eat?
It's true

I wouldn't be
out here
and sweating

as I work
the brittle earth
to yield its food.


And the mother
of my future sons
would be no mother,

suffering to bear
our tender babies.
The things I know

that you would otherwise
have kept from me!
How to shape

my independence
from the earth itself
by struggling

in its furrows;
how to *love*
what can be lost

and does not live
forever; how to cleave
to *her*

in act and not just *word*,
to simultaneously
divide and unify

her body
as flesh of my
flesh and bone

of my bone;
and how to wonder
whether it was we

who fed ourselves
on that sweet fruit
that suckled us

together –
or *You*, who,
knowing all

and capable
of doing all,

spread – long before

the light
first cleaved the depths
of darkness,

and other creatures
swam and crawled
and flew –

the net
whose filaments,
so unavoidable,

would set us free
from You.

# Cain' s Regret

I am not terrified
out here, alone,
far from my parents'

home
and all that I
have known;

nor am I frightened
at the act
of fervor

that crushed
my brother's skull
so that he'll never

rise again –
the truth is,
angry as I was,

as jealous
of the blithe,
untrammeled
and self-righteous way

in which he brought his gifts
and saw the Lord
accept them,

and sorry
as I am no longer
to cross words

with him,
my *brother*:
to watch the sun

go down together
and wonder
with the passion

of our ignorance
if it would rise
again

(and each time
it came up,
no matter when and how

it fell to earth –
as I predicted
and he, till dawn

denied) –
I don't regret
the moment

when I struck him down...

but curse myself

that, knowing

that I was guilty
of a crime
I could not know

would be a crime
(how many times
had I knocked him down
before,

in heated arguments?
He surely should have
stood again
aglow with red at dawn),

I lied

and did not say
"I did
what could be justified."

It is that lie
that gripes me;
my failure

to take responsibility
for that one deed
that sets me now

adrift.

# Sarah' s Lament

*"And Abraham took the wood for the burnt-offering, and laid it upon Isaac his son; and he took in his hand the fire and the knife; and they went both of them together... and Abraham dwelt in Beersheba... And Sarah died in... Hebron... and Abraham came to mourn for Sarah, and to weep for her... and... buried Sarah, his wife, in the cave of the field of Machpelah..."*

—Gen 22:6, 19 and 23:2, 19

On that cold autumn morning,
I never realized
that I would never see
either one of them again.

I felt my husband
stir and rise
while darkness hovered,

and, half-awake,
half still dreaming,
I heard him call

gently
to Isaac,
who responded with surprising

ease,
and I heard them
leave the tent,
together.


Later, when my senses
were fully *there*
and bearing

my morning tea
out to the dawn,
I scanned

the distant hills
toward Moriah,
and I understood

that he had also taken
our two best
servant boys

and our finest mule.
By the cooking fire
I shivered,


and not from the cold,
when I saw
the empty space

where my sharpest,

largest kitchen knife

was no longer
bound in its place.



Too many days later,
toward evening,
one of the boys arrived

as a messenger
from my husband,
to inform me

that all was well
with him

and with Isaac,
my son,

safe, after events
that even the lad

who waited patiently
at the foot of the mountain,
could only surmise.

Father and son, together,
offered a ram,
it seems,

to the mighty God,
the invisible force,
the voice

that has commanded
Abraham
since before we were wed.

My son
is safe
with his father,

in Be'ersheva,
the messenger reported.


Yet, as suddenly
I have begun to feel
the weight of my years,

I find myself
consumed by questions.


*Four*, to be precise:

What *really* happened

on that mountain peak—
so awful that my husband

never returned to me?

How have he and Isaac fared,
after that moment,
without my mediating
presence to

bind them
together?

Will I see them again,
ever,
before some cave-like

burial site
swallows me?

Is all the pain
that I have felt
since that fateful dawn—

forgotten by Abraham
who once thought me
so beautiful,

that he shamed himself
before
the pharaoh in Egypt;

torn from my beloved Isaac,
my song and my laughter,

my one
and only son,
whom I love

as far as the farthest star
and back again

—as fully as the desert
is full of sand:

is my pain a punishment
sent from my husband
and his God

for forcing Abraham
to send away
that Egyptian handmaiden,

Hagar,
and Ishmael,
her son?

# Abraham's Secret Query

*"And Isaac took her into his mother Sarah's tent; and he took Rebecca and she became his wife and he loved her; and Isaac was comforted for [the loss of] his mother."*

— Gen 24:77

When Eliezer
brought her back
all the way from Haran,

it was true that Isaac felt
a certain calm
enter his soul

as she entered
his tent—a counterweight
to the lost weight

of his dead mother.

I *saw* that,
just as I knew that
the story now was *his*.

But I, even *with* Keturah,
had been the lonely one
for so *long*—ever since

I led my son straight up
God's mountain
without hesitation

in that solemn march at dawn.


Sarah was lost to me
from that moment
until I returned.
much later,

to bury her.

I had sent away
Hagar and Ishmael

and felt a tornness
when God's word came again
to me:


Isaac was all that I had left—
*Isaac*, whose life pushed me
to abandon my first-born.

*Isaac understood*

the silent voice
commanding me,

as we ascended the precipice,

but he left me
when I left him,
unbounded,

at the threshold
of his mother's tent,
as I journeyed on alone.

> So now
> that tent is filled
> with lush and lithe
>
> *Rebecca*.
>
> *I* commanded my servant
> to bring that daughter
> from our tribal distance
>
> to wed my son
> so that my bloodline
> would continue
>
> in its sacred purity.

Alas, I shall not

see their children,
the gentle offspring

of Isaac and Rebecca,
playing at my feet

—for our line awaits
so *long* the progress
of our generations.

        We are *different*.

        I, who was the last
        man in
        my tribe

        to offer his son
        to his God—

am I the first man

to crave the presence
of my daughter-in-law
within my bed?

# Isaac Reminisces

The two things
I remember
about that day

that drove
an endless dart
between my parents'

love
was this:
my father's fear

(he called it "awe")
of saying "no"
to that dark voice

I also hear,
                    so that he took me
                        and the wood

                        and blade
                    and journeyed
                to that distant hill

                without a question
                without a pause

without a hint of hesitation

to offer *me*,
the final fruit
of his old age,

(and I kept pace
with his decision);
and, two,

my mother's rage
at father's madness:
"what father

takes his son
his only son
still left

and leaves
on such a voyage?
That crazy man

without a heart
or hope!"
she raved.

They both had laughed
before my birth
in disbelief

that I'd come forth.

That I exist
is proof

of how the voice
is real,
that brought my parents

a son
when cold with years,
and helped my mother

make my father
send away the one,
my half-hewn brother

who would frighten me
when we still played
together,

that took me
to the hills
and brought me back from there.


I do remember

two clear things
about that day:
my mother's rage

when I returned

at dusk
and told her

where we'd been;
my father's terror
of the fire

of her eyes
and voice
that filled our tent

until the day
when, with her death,
she stilled his fear

and he came home
to bury her.


I am now
as he was then:
well-stuffed with days

and nights
that seem colder
then they were

when my two sons,
still young, contended
between tent and track.

I cannot see
as well as I recall
the coming of Rebecca

and how I loved her then –
and love her still,
with all the madness

over which bright son
will save our future.
I shall *not* fear

her rage, who will *not* rage
at my decision
to offer blessings

to them, each
as he should seek it
and receive:

the final fruit
brought forth from me –
the Voice that speaks it,

through my own,
is joined to our eternity.

# Samson's Last Thoughts

They all think
that I am simply stupid,
a muscled brute
with hardly a brain

who sways back
and forth between
hate for the Philistines
and lust for their women.

They do not know
my secret—I do not mean
my seven curling locks
of hair

but what they symbolize:
my special covenant
with God
whose spirit

fills my earthen limbs
with more than normal
strength and speed.

They'll never know
that my weakness
wasn't woven
of well-fleshed women

and that I knew
who might and who
might not betray me.

Could I, who posed
that clever riddle—
when leaving a young lion
torn apart with my bare hands

and scooping up the honey
from its deconstructed jaws,
and knowing that my wife
gave them, my wedding guests
and enemies, the answer—
be so *blind,*
or with the constant prodding
of Delilah, awakening

each time that she tried out
the lies I told her
about my power
and failed: how

could I fail to see
that she, too, would
betray me
if I gave her

what she wanted?
No, I was not
that unaware.

My secret, my strength
and weakness and the source
of my immortal death
is wrapped in other cloth:

I had grown weary
of the charade
of misplaced hate
and lust, not love,

and more,
of the *responsibility*
of that covenant,
of my role as superstar

athlete extraordinaire
and protector of my people,
and of the burden of God's spirit
breathing always within

and around me. I wanted
to be *free* of it
and perhaps, perhaps, to see
what I could do, Godlessly alone

and as an ordinary man.
And it may be,
I will admit,
that I was wrong

to give away my gift
so easily. Blind as I became
I gained a further sight
into this world

of politics and war
between our peoples
and our genders—
with our God-given

will to be free, not
knowing that there are no
freedoms without burdens
in *this* life, at least.

And as my eyes grow darker
my hair grows longer
and I grow stronger,
silently—they think me
not just stupid but still

weak, these Philistines.
Silently I call, now,
upon the God I tried to leave
but who only turned away

from me temporarily,
to restore the power
to my arms and chest and legs
and belly as I offer

to my hosts one last
entertainment: that with me,
they die, laughing.

# II. Ancient Greeks and Romans

# Before the "Fallen Warrior of Aegina"

"...and before moving on toward the exit, do note, ladies and gentlemen, how this magnificently carved, life-sized figure—placed so that it perfectly fits the frame created by this particular section of pediment on the early fifth-century BCE Temple of Aphaia (on the island of Aegina)—is exquisitely formed from all sides, although it would actually only be seen from the front, and how even dying, the anonymous warrior retains that expression with upturned lips known as 'the Archaic smile.' This will conclude our tour of the highlights of Munich's *Glyptotek*."


You haven't moved
in twenty-five centuries,
awkward as it is

to lean forever
on that left arm,
the tendons stretched,

the sinews bulging,
the muscles still
intact and firm

but silently
strapped
into the perfect circle

of marble carved as bronze
and ox hide,

layers tautly pulled

against layers
to sustain you
through the millennia

as they did not
during the battle
that brought you to this

endless moment.
Awkward as it is,
you maintain your pose,

as if it were your field
position, and you
still follow

the captain's orders,
not subsiding
into death.

Awkward as it is,
you do not slip
one centimeter

from your appointed
pedimental place.
Your right arm

clings
without life
and yet without release

to the sword

that did its work
but not quite well enough,

which now, forever,
counterbalances
the rhythm

of that other arm
and pressure of that shield
and the diagonalizing drift

of your legs
left each
to find

its own direction.
Are the muscles
of your torso tense

in pain
or in the godlike community
of strength

that has not waned
in two millennia
and more

since strength failed you?

What can I tell
of who you were

from eyes
hidden by the
unyielding stony helmet

that, in spite of its
gravity, its ponderous
weight upon your head

has never shifted down
your face,
has never scraped

your straight unbroken
nose and can't occlude
that strange smile?


Whose body
did those eyes caress
on the evening

before you journeyed
out to your last battle?
Whose eyes,

in turn,
stroked hungrily your
muscled manliness?

Did someone's
fingers slip
among the hairs

now darkened by
your helmet?
Did you *know*

love
and say so
with your mouth

in words
or smiles
or kisses?

That smile
shows no pain,
but neither does it manifest
the pleasure

that you might have felt, once

or that you might
feel now
at being

an immortal
of sorts,

at being
what even Akhilleus
was not—

solid and unwraithlike—
when Odysseus found him
in the portal

to that Other world,
opened  through the skilled
counsel of a goddess.

That smile
curves in understanding,
that life is both
forever—

as long,
at least, as men
make war

and love

and build

houses of memory
in which they place

the solid monuments
of our evanescence—

and swiftly
gone,
when measured
by flesh,

not stone,
and breath
that moves

in and out
in war
and love,

instead of hovering
in stagnant stillness
and speaking in silences—

that falls,
awkward as it may be,
when the time to fall

has come,


that sings
and sighs
and is recalled, perhaps,

with tears
and dark-hued dirges
that dry

and fade
into the night air
as the sun slides down

beyond our grasp,
and there is no one alive
who remembers

your glorious name.

# "The Penthesilea Painter": Akhilleus In Love

*"The anonymous painter of bowl 2688 in Munich (ca 470-60
BCE) depicts Achilles, in Attic red-figure style, slaying the
Amazon queen, Penthesilea. It is the first time in the history of
this art form that the eyes of two protagonists meet—perhaps
reflecting a tradition that Achilles fell in love with her at the
moment his sword entered her."*

— A History of
Greek Vase Painting

Who would have thought
that I would love

a woman –
not a slave

to serve my bed,
but one with spirit

like a man:
an amazon,

whose fellow
warrior-girls,

they say,

devour men,

and leave no trace
except in offspring

as their
bitter legacy?

If *only* they had fought
against the woman-stealing

Trojans! Instead of being enemies
they would have battled

by my side. She,
Penthesilea, queen

of warrior-women,
might have hunted

in the shadow of my shield;
her arrows

and my spear
would have found their mark

together,
bringing many a prey

to earth.
At night

we might have
kept each other

entertained with tales
of valorous events

and warm
as the camp fires waned

toward dawn
and our new conquests.

Perhaps
my hollow ships

would have steered her home
to my father's careful farm

where we might even
have grown old together,

full of years
and children.

Perhaps somehow
and somewhere else –

but not before the brazen
gates of Ilion,

where *now*,
when it is late

for such a rush
of thoughts,


I plunge my sword
into my beauteous enemy

and meet her eyes
with mine

and understand
her courage that I love,

the noble resignation
to her fate

to cease
to live

—as *I* will
ere this city falls

and all my ships
sail full toward home

without me.

# Father and Son: *Nostoi*

"Nostoi *are homecoming epics—the most renowned and only fully surviving example is the* Odyssey—*deriving from the Greek root* nost-, *meaning "home." (Since the root* alg- *means "pain," 'nostalgia' is 'pain for home'). Agamemnon and Menelaos both made it home, the one to Mykenae and the other to Sparta, but Agamemnon was slaughtered by his wife, Klytaimnestra, who ensnared him in a net while he was bathing and stabbed him to death—no doubt to avenge his sacrifice of their daughter, Iphigenia, although she had also taken a lover, Aigisthos, during her husband's long absence—leaving the unhappy task to their son, Orestes, of avenging his father's death. We know of this through the trilogy of plays by Aiskhylos, collectively known as the* Oresteia."*

—A Commentary on Greek Epic and lyric Poetry

## I *Agamemnon Ruminates upon Arriving toward Mykenae*

The whole, long voyage
home
I kept wondering:

did I do the right thing –
to pay such costs –
of ten long years

away
from these majestic walls,

that dominate an immortal view,

these rough-hewn ramparts and
wine-stained halls
of echoing stone,

and the tales they hold,
peaceful, watchful Mykenae –

to have left all *this*
to battle for a woman
and not my own?

So many noble men,
their souls swallowed
by the three-headed dog,

their bodies birds' food
and canine plunder
and ashes.

Oh, Akhilles,
splendid, golden Akhilleus!
by far the best of us –

and I, so foolish
to have tried to take your prize;
if you could only hear me now,

I'd tell you that I really do
regret the insult. I'd
serve a man owning

nothing, give up being king
of all this,
for a time,

to atone...
That you should have gone down,

and  Aias after you,
so loyal, so sturdy – like my own
Mykenae's stone...

Old friend, Odysseus,
wise and wily –
we would have all

been lost,
bleating for our wives
when Helen licked the wooden horse's

belly with those honeyed tones,
had you not recognized a ruse
and stilled us –

now *you* are lost
devoured somewhere
by Poseidon's wrath.


I think sometimes,
even of the handsomeness
of Troy

with question and with grief:
to bring to dust
and ash

such fine-built towers,
and the warrior-sons within them...
Poor Hektor

deserved a better fate,
and certainly his infant son
should not –

well, who knows, though,
had we let him live,
*when* this bitter cycle

would have ended?
but oh, the pain
I feel at times

— for my *own* progeny:

was it really worth
the sacrifice
of Iphigenia

to sail, to gain immortal
glory
and much plunder,

to lead the blood-
and gore-infested troops
(although I must admit

the taste of it
appealed to my
warrior-heart). But

was her life
for my unchallenged leadership

a fair exchange? I ache
when I think of her soft

face, her young neck

offered without question
to her father's blade,
after the deception

that she would be Achilles' bride...


I did what
I *had* to do –
I did what

the goddess
and my troops
and the future

of the enterprise
which I was leading

required of me.
As a soldier,
I left my heart

and my daughter's life
aside. Perhaps – who knows?
she and the warrior share

the same bright corner, now,
of Elysium...


But I am *home*,
I have returned, at last,

with body and soul

intact,
and that's the *irony*:
so many greater men than I

and Menelaos
are dead,
yet *we* two both *survived,*

he, to bring fair-girdled Helen
back,
and I

to return to loving,
doting Klytemnestra,
who surely missed me

as these walls did,
as I did them.
That blood-red carpet –

or really,
wine-dark, royal purple –
that she laid out

for me:
how caring!
No doubt the gods

will forgive my
not-quite proper
passage along

its plush path,
*before*, not *after*

I have been purged

of the journey's
woes.
It was so long,

the voyage,
and surely they will wait
and eagerly accept

the offerings
prepared for them
once I have been cleansed

by the steam-hot
bath
prepared for me

by my wife's own hand.

## II *Orestes Steels Himself*

It is only you,
Pylades,
who will truly know –

surely not
Elektra,
whom I know you'll wed,

whom you must never tell,
who fears her mother's

will as if

it were divine;
and surely not the ghost
of Agamemnon,

my father now long gone
who left me here
when he

went forth
to find his name,
and back
to find his fate

at mother's hand,
(he left me twice, then) –

you alone, Pylades,
will *know*

that, when I finally

twist the bronze
into my mother's
iron breast,

cold metal
against cold
metal

— when blood pours out,
far thicker, and, yes, sweeter
then that milk

I scarce recall –

it will not be
my father's murder
I avenge,

for whom his children
were no more than instruments

of immortality.

It is true

that gods and men
expect a son
to kill his father's

killer,
even if that be
his mother,

but gods possess
forever and unquestioning

the portion
that is theirs;

they cannot be bereft
of rights and home
and patrimony,

and cannot feel
the pain of exile.
They do not *know*

what I know

of loss – a transformation
from childhood

to being a man
without a man
to guide me,

the loss
of love
for years,

cast out
by my mother
and her lover,

deprived of all
that should have been
my own.


The gods are not
omniscient
who will never know

that I slay
my father's slayer
not for him

and his pale shade
but for myself,
to appease my furious

anger
because of what she took
from *me*

and can't give back
unless I *take* it back:

the throne,
the fawning courtiers,
the power over my life

and others'
and all the love
that comes with home

that shall be mine
when with her death

I still my hatred.

# The Poet's Last Words

"Homer was universally regarded by the ancients as the author of the two great poems, the *Iliad* and the *Odyssey*. Such continued to be the prevalent belief until the year 1795, when the German professor, F.A. Wolf, wrote his *Prolegomena*, in which he endeavored to show that the *Iliad* and the *Odyssey* were not two complete poems, but small, separate epic songs, celebrating single exploits of the heroes and that these lays were written down and united, as the *Iliad* and the *Odyssey*, by Pisistratos. This opinion gave rise to a controversy regarding the origin of the Homeric poems which is not yet settled and which probably never will be... The *Odyssey* was composed after the *Iliad*, and many maintain that they are the works of different authors..."

*—from* Sir William Smith:
*Smaller Classical Dictionary*

Someday,
hundreds of years from now
—thousands,

if the glory of my words
is truly undying—

the bookmen,
of dull mind,

(who substitute their sullen
study of the text
for inspiration

of  just the sort
with which the gods
swallow up my kind

and spew forth
through us
well-wrought epics

of their deeds
and those of men)—

the bookmen will wonder,
as they wander
through the multitude

of dactyls
I have created
(almost endless

rows of them—arrayed
like a catalogue
of ships that, poised

in the silent harbor
at Aulis,
waiting for the goddess

to relent,
when suddenly
the winds begin to fly

and the wine-dark
depths of ocean

spew forth froths of foam

and salt-sweet,
swiftly-flowing, crested
smooth-bellied liquid hillocks,

and the rejoicing voices
of men and birds alike
are carried far

into the glowing dawn,
—like such ships going boldly forth
to navigate

explosively,
excitedly
the waves toward Troy

or some other destination:
just so my words array themselves)

—they'll ask if I am truly
the master poet

of so many words

so finely carved
out of the infinite range
of god-hewn syllables,

harnessed to the patterns
oft prescribed by those
whose sounds preceded mine

and fed my ears
and filled my mind
from before the time

I even knew
that my outer eyes
were not seeing

what they would never see,

for the worlds I saw
and ever see
through the gods' gift

and turn
upon my tongue
in almost endless re-

vision, compensates:

indeed my eyes

perceive
the heroes

and their agonies,
the glorious names


that I have given them
in warring with their pain
and singing

of their mighty feats
with spears and swords and stones
along the Trojan plain

and of their boundless hopes:
those words will live

'til songs are gone
and words are done...

The bookmen will ask
and argue

—like Thersites
upon the beach,
questioning the ways

and wiles of Odysseus—

whether I contrived

the epics

that they must read
who can no longer chant
from memory
much less create
from masses of mere words
as I have.

They'll spew forth
tales fashioned
of catalogues of

notes—as many as
the warriors who sailed forth
to rescue Helen

and were lost.

They'll speculate:
if he wrote *one*

Did he also write
the *other*? As if
a poet filled

with voices from the gods
could not speak twice:
once with bronze and oxhide

beaten

like the weaponry
breathed into being

by Hephaistos
and suitable
for Ares

or Athene,
and once
with the fury

of the sea
and the cleverly-woven
threads of a never-ending

tapestry,
words woven by an Aphrodite
whose ever-changing beauty

brings home
the errant warrior,
the hero who receives

and gives
much pain
and deathless

centuries of pleasure.

These queries

will possess them.
Am I one

or am I two
or am I many
or none at all,

they'll never cease
from wondering.
These, and many more matters

will preoccupy them,
regarding bronze and iron tripods
and the varied modes of delivering

the dead
to the underworld
and how it was—

*if* it was at *all*
as I sing it—
that I could *know*

so much
so well
to sing

so flawlessly.
Some may even think

that the wily one

himself deceived
the Phaiakians

who would bear him home,
with words
I placed

upon his lips:
that all the ogres
were not *there*

beyond the outer boundaries
of the ocean's flow
and deep within its secrets,

that he was merely
*entertaining* them
with noble-sounding

falsities
(and then: am *I*
the author of such lies

or *he*? they'll ask.)


But if the honest
ordering of my words
should bring me

*immortality*,
so that, like light-limbed Hermes,
my verses soar

across the endless sky
of time
and skim, as that god does,

the surface
of all the surging seas
one might imagine,

then the readers who come
well after me,
devoid of heart

but filled
with minds
that question

as they plod,
will never *know*,
will not suspect

the truth.


*For twenty years
she waited*

and still, it seemed,

she waited more
for him

to hasten back
scarred with glory
and the sacred gore

of that great war.

For twenty years
she watched her son

grow up without a father near
as she, too, feared
that she'd grow old

without a man to share
her bed,
her thoughts,

her hopes.

For twenty years
they clamored
for her hand

and for her body
and her wealth
and she, lest she grow cold,

opened

up and closed again
the story

of the heroes' acts
upon her loom
close by the fire

in the well-swept
hearth
of her well-kept room.


But not alone:

by day, between
the stunted swords
of the ugly, arrogant suitors

she spoke of him
with words and warp
and weft

as I did, too,
pursuing him
with my mind's eye

as he wandered
from the Kyklops
to the sorceress,

and watched his loyal men

get swept away
and wept

before Kalypso's cave
when he awoke
to think of homecoming

after seven years
within her womb.
I followed him to the edge

of earth,
the very gates
of the other world

and listened
through his ears
to the voices

of Akhilleus and Teiresias
and others,
and willed him back

at last,
but *only* when
*my* appetites were sated

for wine from Ithake
and fat-fleshed flocks
and worlds passed through

by means of
his adventure—

and the wife he left behind
with whom, by night,

I wove another story
never to be told,
of passion

borne to and from
a poet whose mouth
and hands

and other parts
must substitute for eyes
that never see

the slowly sinking
flesh,
the tiny wrinkles

engraved
by time's
long finger nails;

we interwove
a passion
perfect, sweet

and as ephemeral,
(as twenty years

most surely *are*
when pushed against
the weight of so many

centuries of unslaked fame),
and fragile
as a textile

that is unwoven
night by night,

leaving no tale
and almost no trace.

# Antigone' s Last Letter to Her Fiancé

*" ...and Oedipus, self-blinded, fled Thebes for the wilderness, cursing the children who fled his presence—save one daughter, Antigone—and doomed his sons (who were his half-brothers) to fight each other and to perish for the throne briefly warmed by Kreon. Kreon decreed that one son be buried and the other not, but Antigone could not allow her unburied brother's soul to languish without the ritual that would carry it to Hades, so she broke Kreon's law and was condemned by him to die..."*

—*on Sophokles'* Antigone (*anon.*)

Haemon,
You were so sweet

to argue with your father
on my behalf.

I *do* love you,
my husband soon-to-be.

But understand
that that may never

happen *here*: for I have
abrogated

Kreon's law,

and we both know
how much his fear

of being questioned, doubted,
contradicted,

ensnares his mind.
He is an older man

and thus afraid
of younger men

– even a loving son –
and oh, the gods do know,

of *women*. He fears
the loss of his

authority
and so rejects

the thoughts of common folk,
as one who was himself

a commoner,
twice raised

to kingly status
through the royal foibles

of *my* family.

Oh, Haemon,
he will see me dead

and even you, perhaps,
before he bends

before the natural winds
of true justice.

I had no choice.
I had to bury *both*

my brothers,
in spite of his command.

I loved my father first

of all men
ever in my life:

my clever father,
with his limp

and his furious temper
and his riddle-making wit!

Oedipus so doted on me,
and spoiled me with gifts

that I could hardly think
of another man

when I came of age –
I preferred, indeed, to follow dad

into his self-imposed exile
(which brought *your* father
into power first).

The only other men who held
my heart

as time grew up with me
were both my brothers,

childhood playmates
so like my dad

in *all* those ways
a son

is like his father.

Imagine

how I dreamed
through them

of what my father was

in youth,

arriving here to Thebes,
a hero

fit for mother's
royal throne

and bed.

Who would have thought

that they'd be kings
who'd argue intermittency

to death?
(And so your father

stretched again
to fit the ruler's seat.)


All that is past,
some of it recent,

my dear Haemon,
and little bits of joy

are all that stay with me:
the memories

of a most extraordinary
childhood and

growing up,
so unaware of all the taints

that soon emerged,
provoking taunts

of those who once admired us.
No man would have me

nor I them –
until you turned my way,

that is,
and asked me

for my hand.
(who else was left to ask for it?)

I shall be always grateful
for your wish to fill

the hole
left by the deaths

of father and my
brothers.

I shall praise you

with the breath

that fills me
all my life

and bury myself
in gratitude

for what you've done
for me

and serve you
as a wife,

as well,
whose only flaw will be –

if knowing this,
you'll still have me –

that my heart only

burns with fire
as for my dearest, loyal

friend –

but  not the lover
you desire.

# Monologue:
# Medea's Journey Home

It was their little faces
that I couldn't bear to see,

that, so sweet and innocent,
almost saved them,

but finally killed them,
because I knew

that boys will become men
as men will be boys

in the troubled end
of every epic voyage...

but more, it was that
every nuance of their

faces cried out his name.
*Jason*'s lips –

deceitful as they held mine once
and as they spewed forth later lies

about our future

and their future

with his new children, soon, to come
from her –

my finger traced
on their sweet mouths.


*Jason*'s straight, unyielding nose
I saw

achieving center
of one son's face

and Jason's ears
stood out

from his little brother's head.
Those eyes like the light

at dawn,
when the sun

has just burst forth
beyond the crags

of Colchis,
with which my Jason

beguiled my will

back there and then,

so that we slew
the dragon, both, together –

those eyes I kissed
I kissed again, in duplicate,

obsidian below the brow
of one,

blue ice
the other.

They share his dark
curls.

They gesture, even now,
as he does

and stand and walk
and shift expressions

as if his seed alone
produced them,

(as if I merely held them
in my womb

until the Greek
would claim them

from his barbarian
princess), as he

forgot that I was royalty,
and sophistry negated my own loyalty

but not my sorcery.


His sons don't see *me*
but only mother

to yield to *need* – they
are so like him

within, without.
The thought of life without him

and with them,
constant mirrors

of his being
and his inconstancy

I could not bear.

And so I slew them.

And really, had I not
– I *know* their future –

and what
would be their lot:

the step-sons
of his new, young wife,

a threat to her
new family.

Treated badly, they
would no doubt end

away from life,
if not its pleasures.

I saved them that.
I couldn't bear

the thought that they
would be

like me, now drawing nigh
to Athens

in a chariot winged
by granddad's dragons:

hovering
between

heaven and earth –

to live
and die

alone
with neither true

human fellowship
nor Olympian power

to comfort
*me*.

# Brutus Reminisces on the Way to Philippi

*"…and you, too, my son?!?.."* –Julius Caesar's last words, *according to Suetonius, directed toward Brutus, the last to stab him in the assassination effected on the Ides of March. The murder was intended to save the Roman Republic from what the assassins believed to be Caesar's desire to subvert the republic and to make himself sole ruler.*

It was near the end
of the two-faced
month

that I last conversed
with him.
As always,

so like a father
to me,
Caesar spoke

in calm
and loving tones,
as if to reassure me

against the fear
he somehow heard
with inner ears

stirring
deep within me.

A double fear
in fact
was what I felt:

that he
had finally
determined

to subvert entirely
the very system
of democracy,

the people's thing
—*res publica*—

that he had served
and surely saved
so many years before

when Pompey
threatened
(or so it seemed)

to lead his troops
against the law
into our Italy.

Later—still
it feels
so long ago—

Caesar decimated
Pompey's army
at Pharsalos

way off in Greece,
and that once-great
one fled

to Egypt,
where his friends
of old

received him
and then slew him.
Now the man

who fought
against a tyrant's
aspiration,

winning Rome's
eternal
gratitude

and its strong
affection
has stood

as consul
for too many years.


That he will
somehow
deconstruct

the senate,

secret of
the polity's

success,
and make himself
Imperator

I fear.
It is a kind of
Rubicon

he must not cross.
And, two,
that if I am to save

the vast
republic—
large enough

that the sea,
that inland
waterway,

is nearly
circumvented
by our lands—

the only course,
if Caesar
makes himself

a *tyrannos:*
an autocrat,
assumes the consulship

for life,

may be to take
his own—

to kill
the man
to whom

I am so like
a son.
As if

he sensed this
double fear
this twice-born struggle

as January
looked both toward the past
and toward today,

he said to me:
"I have decided,
I am most certain,

that now that
Rome
the city

—and the nearly
endless
stretch of lands

that she commands—
is stable,
I must

step down

from my position
of consul's

power
and pass
the role

of governance
to those
whose youth

can lead us
to the future.
New Men

as I myself
once was.
Perhaps

I might retain
the place
of Pontifex

Maximus, my
duties thus confined
to guarding

Roman piety
in the performance
of my sacred duties.


But I will leave
the field of politics
as I have left behind

the field of battle
since conquering Gaul
and Britain

and Pompey,
once called Great.
Oh, Brutus,

my favored son,
I would propose
that you

and Marcus Antony,
stand next
as consuls

come the
vernal equinox,
and the cycle

of new senate
choices is announced.
I will proclaim

my clear intent
to end my consulship
on March 14th,

a week before
the earth
and sun

will match
our ordered world
in shifting

that long ratio
of day to night
and dark to light.

And if, my gallant
one, I fail
to follow

my own words,
take this,
*my* knife,

whose blade
has felt the blood
of all too many

enemies
of Rome.
Use it, my son,

and take my life
before two days
have passed,

and be
the savior
of the state."

Wordless
did I listen
and mindless

did I feel
and numb
as I was hurrying

late that evening
to the home
of Cassius

to inform him
of this conversation
and to shape

another plan
that offers hope
that we might bring

the Roman world
back to its roots
in piety

and people's
passion
for community

and not
that single *self*-ruled
preference

that brought
the end
to Athens' glorious inventions

and threatens
Rome and all
its virtuous

intentions.

# III. Time Between Time

# ASTROLABE'S SECOND COMMUNION

It is so cold here
on this Breton coast
where they have left me
to be raised by others.

The wind persecutes
my bones
every grey winter
while I wait for them.
And in the summer,
that very wind
carrying the gull-borne sun,
sears my flesh.


It is so lonely here,
surrounded by flocks
of well-intentioned
dark and pitiless nuns,
so wary of letting me
understand
who I am.


I know them,

who my parents are:
*Abelard and Heloise* –
the occasional word let slip
throughout the past twelve years
informs my curiosity
with fragments
of the love that melted them
as one
and also tore them
from themselves
and from me.

Scholars, I surmise,
he the brilliant, she
the more so,
if those slivered words
are true—

and this I find
the more so unbelievable:
my mother, smarter,
who was, of course,
a woman
like the women
who have nurtured me

in this cauldron
of coldness
with their dull
and hollowed-out
loneliness.

Was he as handsome as
they sometimes say,
in whispers,
when they think I cannot hear?

Did he look like me, once —
and what of her?
I find the passion
I infer for my mother
from my father
unimaginable:
the only
picture I sustain
is reflected in the mirror
of these parchment-skinned
poor sisters
who dog my days
with useless histories
and the ways
of God.


I have heard
of the great Saint,
Bernard, whom I think
a scoundrel,
all too willing
to soak my dad
in scandal,
devoid of mind

and jealous
of those who love
their God with logic.
May his crusade
to end the world
of thought,
of Abelard
be not the only one
that ends
in grief!

Is he the one
because of whom
they chose
to leave me here
for lo these many years?

Will they turn back
to each other
and bring me forth
to the gilded city
where they first met?

Or did they name me
*Astrolabe*,
because they knew
in all they knew
that I would someday, too,
learn to turn
my harrowed eyes

toward the cold and blistering stars
to find my own way
home
in this sea

without them
needed now
to guide me?

# BEFORE GINEVRA

*"...and in the next gallery we shall find the only painting by Leonardo da Vinci in the United States, a stunningly delicate portrait of Ginevra da Benci, framed by juniper branches—a pun on her name ('Ginevra' means 'juniper,' in Italian). Along the peripheral walls are portraits of various young men; three in front of the Leonardo, done by Andrea del Sarto, Sandro Botticelli, Fillipino Lippi, and two somewhat toward its back (which is inscribed, by the way, with the words* virtutem forma decorat, *meaning 'beauty adorns virtue,' wrapped around a juniper branch and flanked by laurel and palm branches), by Lorenzo di Credi and The Master of Santo Spirito. Two portrait busts by Rosselini, representing the young John the Baptist, and two by Desiderio da Settignano, fill out the gallery... Please take a few moments to gaze into Ginevra's extraordinary eyes and admire her smooth, pale face; I will be waiting in the gallery directly across the Great Hall, to continue our visit with Franz Hals and other seventeenth-century Dutch portrait masters..."*

They surround you,
Ginevra,
these acolytes,

devotees of your beauty
and virtue,
desiring

more, to be

suitors of your
love.

They stare

as they have been staring
for so long
it seems like centuries,

eternity, even:
but your graceful
mien

conjures endless adoration.
They want to be closer,
to be *with* you—

to be *like* you...
the way a lover sees the world
through his lover's eyes—

almost, then, to *be* you,
just as their fathers
would surely kill

to be *your* father.
Desiring eyes
can't kill, of course—

except, perhaps,
*yours*, so delicate,

by way of swooning

calmness. If eyes
could kill, if cupid's
arrows were sharp enough,

your pale pink cheeks
might well be swathed
in darker red,

shot from men's desire, your
rose-petal lips
parted in soft pain,

your white brow
turned red--
like the cloak

enveloping
Andrea's son,
who would transfix you,

if he could,
with his haughty,
almost hostile sneer,

his dark eyes dominating
the broken nose
and upturned lips

and strange-shaped ears

and crimson garment
with which he fails

to turn your stunning face
toward his.

Across the way, sweet Sandro's son
tries to draw your eye

by holding out
that bright medallion—
as if the antiquated image

of the saint
who thrice denied
his master's overpowering love

could pull your heart
toward his, in sympathy
for that unworthy passion,

poignant in its
frailty: Sandro's son's for you,

the saint's love
for his God.

Or perhaps he hopes,
impressed by the ancient

artifacts that he commands

—the golden medal
scintillating in the light,

a mirror for your
hazel-golden eyes
and hair,

just *one* of his possessions
offered
as if to tempt you—

you'll turn.
But you don't stir.

Nor do you move
your perfect, placid face

toward the son
of Fillippo, although
the sensuous outlines

of his firm, soft visage
held so vertically erect
were shaped, I'd swear,

as if alone to find *you*;
although his bright red cap
announces to the world

the passion
that he feels for you:

the suffering that he endures

behind the non-emotive
face.

The other noble youths
—Lorenzo's boy and that other—
I shall not speak of:
they lag behind you,

bearing the landscapes
behind their minds
that cannot match

the bluish ground and sky
that drifts behind *you*, the echo
of those criss-crossed bright blue

cords that weave a fence
across your swelling breast,
denying access

to the heart within.

Oh, Ginevra,
how they all do yearn

for you.
(The sons of Rosellini,
recognizing the futility
of their brothers' cause,

just turn their heads
in question: why to *try* to have you?)

They worship you
as if you were a goddess:
a *dark* goddess,

your flesh so pallid,
your halo spilling brown-green
forest sweetness,

juniper leaves, bristling, one by one,
around your face and hair.

But they are all so *clumsy*
compared with you:
their noble forms

are barely crescent moons
when in the ambit
of your sun:

that exquisite nose,
those flower-lips:
it is no wonder

that your dreamy eyes
look elsewhere.

They stare at you,
and you stare *away*...

—and *is* it dreaminess
or just fatigue
—or *fear*—

that  emanates from eyes
that pass right through me,
as *I* take *my* place

as an adorer
among these men?

The hint of dark, rough shadows

starts to show
beneath your eyes,
the evidence of sleepless nights

and days awake;
your endless peering
under heavy lids

now leads my eyes
to follow yours
to see what, past us *all*,

you *see*. Beyond

the portal
of the gallery
where all are gathered,

and through
the rough-hewn light
of that great corridor,

another portal opens,
and placed across from you,
within the time and space

that follow
from one country
to the next,

from Italy, south,
to Holland, north,
she sits, contemplating

you, who stare at *her*.

Her label speaks:
"*Old Woman*,"
(for she was sixty

when *her* father,
Franz, created her).

I understand, now,

when I watch her
watch you,
with a sad smile

stiffly stitched

into a broad face
framed in ruffled lace
and darkness

that are as unforgiving,
as unstinting
in the stark starch

of their truth,
as the skein of age

that webs her face.

The smile,
as it were,
examines you

across the galleries
and eras,
as do her eyes.

All
seems to say:
"I've been there, too.

I was once young
and beautiful
and many men
pursued me.

How can it *be*

that time so swiftly
robbed my flesh
of its plump lushness

—with such alacrity
that I can hardly,
now, recall,

*when* my youthfulness
became old age?"

And you,
Ginevra,

who glow,
and carry virtue in your heart,

possess discernment, too,
within your leaf-crowned head.

You stare at her,
ignoring these inferior
suitors all around, and wonder

and, yes, *worry*
*when* that proper prince
will enter your garden

gate, between the palm

and laurel branches
guarding you—

*how* soon
before that demon,
time, sucks out that smooth,

sweet pinkness
from you,
and *you* become like *her*,

with lips no longer
pursed in fragile
mystery,

but with the well-worn
knowledge
of your own life history

gone by,
your beauty,
once ineffable,

escaped
to where even Leonardo
for all his genius

cannot fetch it back.

# INNER VISION

It is now,
fair Nefertiti,
that, not knowing

why *all* your parts
are as they are--

the strangely
risen crown
that some suggest

withholds a stranger
skull, elongated
not from intellect

but from malady,
by startling contrast,
the stunning chin

the rosebud lips
the proud, straight nose
that dominate

your wondrous visage
poised
on the slender pedestal

of neck--

nor grasping
your sinuously shaped
eyelid,

but the eyes

themselves
I *understand*,
I see why *they* are

as they are.


One stares out,
its onyx pupil

searching
for some future
hope, perhaps

a kindred soul
in another era.
The other, black,

but not *empty*:
it searches, rather,

inwardly for enlightenment
hidden from the rest.

It is *not,*
as most would say,
the damage

of millennia
that left its mark
on your left eye.

I understand this now

as I stare from you
to Modigliani's

Beatrice
and at his Jeanne
and at his concierge's daughter

and the others
with their
serpentine necks

and sharp-edged
chins and noses
and their

eyes:

the right one outward,
the left one inward-
looking,

blurred to us,
seeking that clarity
of vision

that sculptors,
painters
and queens of Egypt

hope to find—
even when the
soulmate, sought

is separated

by aeons and the wide-eyed sea.

# IV. Seasons: Then and Now

# *Recall*

On my 63rd birthday
for some unconjurable reason
I think of the mouth wash
that you used to use
when I was little
and you were
younger
than I am now,

and alive,
father.

You kept the bottle
on the glass shelf
above the sink
with separate
faucets
for cold and hot water
in the private bathroom,
all covered

in small
white,
sun-soaked
tiles,

near your study
that we rarely entered,
fearful
of disturbing you—

but I cannot

remember

the name

of that astringent.

# The Man with the Hose

The man with the hose
pauses
to let me pass

without wetting my shoes
as he greets the morning's
music

by pushing all the butts

and other fragments
of last night's

drinks
and dreams
into the gutter

to let the concrete
gleam
in the sun's reflection.

In those moments
before the water dries,
hurrying to work,

I am suddenly
drenched
with the memory

of you, holding
the hose
on the slick, emerald

grass
on a summer morning
in Maine

so Dafna, Eyton and I
might daringly
wet our naked feet

and even our legs,
so long ago,
when we were

so small
and you were so

alive,

Daddy.

# Hallowe'en

Hallowe'en again
with ghosts
floating through

the streets
at dusk
and as the night

sets in,
the enchanted voices
of children,

giggling, excited
behind their
masks

and costumes.
I watch my eight-year-old,

thrilling
to the gentle
spooks

of autumn's
whistling sounds,
the red-and-golden

billows
carrying off
the hopes

of summer.

Oh, sweet
laughter

webbed with
nascent dreams
for him,

and quickly grown
with memories
of Hallowe'ens

now large
in delighted
recollection,

devouring treats,
dissolving
in the apple air.


I still

remember,

thirty years
ago, (or was it
more?) how

I went
trick-or-
treating

(I was twelve)
and ran off
with my friends

too fast
for you
to follow

(you were eight)
and even though
you came back

later
and so laden
with a wealth

of sweets
and joyful,
giggling as

you dropped
your mask
and poured out

the spoils
of your evening's
venture

—you'd quite
forgotten
that I'd left

you quite
abandoned,
little brother—

I still am
haunted
by that dark

remembered night,
and wonder
if you ever

think
back
to that

evening,
when—if you
have them—you

clothe your
children
to send them out.

# Enkidu

O Enkidu where
have you fallen?
"The earth

reached up
and seized me."
Have you learnt

of the man
having a brother;
have you seen him?

"I have seen him;
one glass
of water

is his portion."

Remember
how we fought
with each other?

and then
my brother
we knew

each other's strength.
We killed
the bull of heaven

together
and slaughtered

the horny slayer

of the city.
The walls
of Urdu

are crumbling, Enkidu,
the high walls
I stopped building

when we fought together.

I have journeyed

over the bitter river
through the rippling
gates of darkness

to find you
and I am lost.
How can I go back

without you?
I have swallowed
water from the river

spilled from the glass
and stained my throat.
I cannot sing

death's lions
overroar me

who cannot sing
alone.

# The Pride of Fatherhood

It was the summer
of '98, when,
pregnant with Brahm

you insisted
that we would need
a car:

a bicycle
could hardly do
for two

when one would be
too fragile
and unable

to pedal for years.
"And it must be
a safe and sturdy car,

whose protective carapace
will serve well
and without
distracting
standard gears,"

you said.
We bought

a Volvo,

solid in its
hideous boxiness,
its starting line energy
opposite to Brahm's:

he's all Maserati,
his limousine is
all Mack truck.


Acknowledging
— and not unhappily
by any means —

that I am *Daddy*, now,
surrounded by a dark
quickly scratched
and swiftly wrinkled badge

of admission
that time moves on
and generations shift

like the manual gears
I sometimes long for,
I move about the city

roads with care
but not the caution,

always, called for

by the precious contents
of my vehicle: not one, indeed,
but by the time

these words
have reached
a reader's eyes,

a second son,
as well —

to say nothing of the pride
with which I pass

a Volvo

*station wagon*,
knowing

that I had strength
to draw the line
in our negotiation

at a black,
automatic
*sedan*.

# Quintessence

There are,
as I reflect
on seasons

and their senses,
and time's elusive moments,

particularized
elements that sing—
patterns
of sweet sounds

that suddenly emerge
out of the phonic chaos,
that cause the heart

to skip
its automatic
round of beats,

to jump
from one pulse
to another,

that pass
or are passed by
too quickly

as we move.


One:
the sussura
of the ocean

on the winter beach
when the ice
moon ripples

at the water's
margin;

two:
the laddered
racket of the birds

in the copper light
before the summer
sun appears;

three: the edge
of wind
that cuts

the trees
that flutter leaves

like endless colored eyelids
when the autumn
sunlight wanes;

four: the surge of rain
enveloping

the daffodils
that seek

as they are soaked
by spring's fulfillment

of their destiny.


Yet more

than these:

the crowded quiet

of midnight darkness,
broken

by the sudden sob of
"Daddy, *come*!"

—in a tiny voice
that summons
from the deepest dreams—

and the blurry calm

sunk into stillness
of his evened breathing

back within his sleep
when soothed,

although
he doesn't know

he feels my fingertips
across his cheek.

# The New Bunk Bed

"It was the bestest
night of my life!"
my five-year-old, Nadav,

exclaims
as he climbs
down from the upper

register of the new
bunk beds we installed
last night for him

and his brother.
I had thought
that it would be

the older one
—a sage and wise child,
months past six—

who would insist
on sleeping in the
stratosphere

of their reshaped room,
but his little brother
was more eager

for that perch.

Like this nearly
ended summer, the
babyhood of both

is dissipating all too fast,
between the heat
of their energy

and still-humid tears
and the bright colors
of their ever-changing,

laughing games.
I confess
that I reveled

in the six
hours of sleep
that fell my way

as their newly appointed
accommodations
embraced them

all night long.


But I will not soon

forget

how, just before I turned
to bed, myself,
I wrapped Brahm's

length within my
arms, to put him back
into the lower

bed—he having
climbed the ladder
to his brother

on this first night
that they slept,
these wondrous boys,

each, alone,

on his own mattress,
with his own
new sheets,

surrounded by separate
animals and toys,

breathing

his own dreams.

# Jungle

There is a jungle,
thick and moist
and towering

beyond the fence
beyond the yard
behind the house

and as the day
wanes from sun
to dusk and night

the light
seeps
through the trees
that flicker without wind

in spots of silver,
gold and emerald.

From my tiny downstairs desk
and quiet window
the view is almost soothing.


Upstairs
my children nap,

their smooth, soft faces
untouched by dreams

of yesterday

or of mortality.

# School Buses

I wonder
where the buses go
each morning
after they disgorge
their little passengers.

Dark and empty
after being stuffed
with laughter
and excited voices
of anticipation,
what do the buses *feel*
as they depart?

Do they have souls
that know
that they are
empty carapaces:
metal and rubber,
black and yellow,
four-wheeled
and simply shaped

but meaningless
when not
the shepherds
of their flocks?

There is a silence
to their motors' roar
as they speed off,

to some huge flat space
beyond the clouded,
crowded streets
where they must wait—

and do they sense
the hours ticking by
until the day will wane
and once again
they heed
the afternoon arriving
with its call to come?

Do they hurry then,
*themselves* once more,
to soar along the routes
toward home,
from school to stop,
to let go
their cargo

bit by bit

until the darkness
covers all
and empty once again—

and then
do they hope,
like every father,
for yet another dawn
exhumed by children,
without knowing
when or whether
it will arrive?

# I Hear the Nightingale in the Tree

...but the nightingale
has no time to waste

for time does not exist for her
nor for the moon

nor for the very earth that turns,
but lo, the turning of my heart

when I think of all the miles
stretched between my love and me

twists
against the days and nights

that, parted from her
are so dark a waste.

# Your Smile

Your smile
ripples
like a road

soaked
in noonday summer
sun.
I wince,

never having been
scalded by a
smile before.

# Late August Evening

The dusk lingers
as if the day,
shrinking, fears to yield,

as crickets and fireflies
have yielded
to cicadas.

The wild cherries
are as plump
as the last tomatoes

and corn are sweet.
Apples,
worm-filled, soak
the tawny grass.

There what once
was dew
is sometimes

frost at dawn.
The heart-shaped leaves
of the beech tree--
the first harbingers--

release their grip
on crooked limbs
preparing

to suck their sap

into their bellies' depths:
another season, reluctantly,

another love,
for naught
but nature's reasons

waning.

# *Fall*

It was a summer
of intense heat,
the sun's passion

soaking deep
into the night,
the very grass

blushing tawny
with exhaustion.
Who would

have imagined
how swiftly and
without explanation

the leaves
would start
to gather

in crumpled, broken
piles in the gutters
and on the sidewalks?

Yellowed flower stalks,
long parched, now chilled,
still hope for rain

that hasn't come.
At night
we need the thick,

down comforter
to keep each other
warm.

# September

The afternoons persist
with sun
that desiccates

the remnants
of the goldenrods
bending above grasses

that no longer struggle
to survive,
unlike hearts

awaiting change.
But the evenings,
sooner at the door than earlier

and grey, wind-swept
dawns
bring sharp edges

to the day,
and presage
windows blurred

with frost.
We hover
between the heat

that still soaks
the neck
and chill that

infiltrates
the floorboards
and lower back

uncertain
as to whether
to remain

or whither to move on.

# November Morning

*(for Warren, in Memoriam)*

From the warmth
of my brightly lit
office on this late
November morning,

the effulgent sunlight
plays, a serrated wind hovering
around those other leaves
that refuse to disconnect
from the nearly empty limbs

of the sugar maple
outside my window.

The dance of light
and shadow
against the ribs
of the screened-in porch
is a fragile, evanescent one,
its patterns a flux of

shapes and rhythms
against the wiry membrane.

Further along the lawn,
thick with unraked
leaves, tree trunks cast
their own reflective shadows
in long, dark lines,
and the newly-placed

sculpture, in white, carved

limestone, dominates
the garden;

beyond it, the fence-gate
yields to the murmuring woods.
There is a young buck,
just now, his fresh-grown
antlers, each with two
sharp points, held aloft

in that pride of youth
and energy that defies
the gathering cold,
calmly nibbling
the remnants

of fading vegetation
from the once-lush grove.


The smooth,
quiet
motion
of this day

spreads
its honeyed
goldness
along the dirt-and-pebble
paths,

its silences

jarred

by the telephone call
that informs me

of your attempted
suicide

and the insistent
questions:

of whether
you will
be here by nightfall
or disconnected,

subsumed into the
darkness that
had already consumed you,

that I somehow never noticed
who watches so intently
as the sun and shadow shape

their fragile choreography
against the ribs and

veils of screened-in spaces.

www.ingramcontent.com/pod-product-compliance
Lightning Source LLC
Chambersburg PA
CBHW051828040426
42447CB00006B/427